SOLVE THAT CRIME!

Crime Under the Microscope!

In the Forensics Lab

Carol Ballard

Enslow Publishers, Inc.
40 Industrial Road
Box 398
Berkeley Heights, NJ 07922
USA

http://www.enslow.com

Library of Congress Cataloging-in-Publication Data

Ballard, Carol.
  Crime under the microscope! : in the forensics lab / Carol Ballard.
    p. cm. — (Solve that crime!)
  Includes bibliographical references and index.
  Summary: "Take a look at how forensics solves crimes in the laboratory"—Provided by publisher.
  ISBN-13: 978-0-7660-3374-0
  ISBN-10: 0-7660-3374-0
  1. Forensic sciences—Juvenile literature. 2. Criminal investigation—Juvenile literature. I. Title.
  HV8073.8.B276 2009
  363.25'62—dc22

                          2008033307

Printed in the United States of America

10 9 8 7 6 5 4 3 2 1

To Our Readers : We have done our best to make sure all Internet Addresses in this book were active and appropriate when we went to press. However, the authors and the publisher have no control over and assume no liability for the material available on those Internet sites or on other Web sites they may link to. Any comments or suggestions can be sent by e-mail to comments@enslow.com or to the address on the back cover.

♻ Enslow Publishers, Inc. is committed to printing our books on recycled paper. The paper in every book contains between 10% to 30% post-consumer waste (PCW). The cover board on the outside of each book contains 100% PCW. Our goal is to do our part to help young people and the environment too!.

For The Brown Reference Group Ltd.
Project Editor: Sarah Eason
Designer: Paul Myerscough
Picture Researcher: Maria Joannou
Managing Editor: Miranda Smith
Editorial Director: Lindsey Lowe
Production Director: Alastair Gourlay
Children's Publisher: Anne O'Daly

Photographic Credits:
Shutterstock: Leah-Anne Thompson front cover; Alamy Images: Ian Miles-Flashpoint Pictures 20; Getty Images: Bentley Archive/Popperfoto 25, Gali Tibbon/AFP 12; Istockphoto: Anji71 35, Christian Anthony 22, Dan Bishop 40, Lorenzo Colloreta 19, Long Ha 9, Kativ 23, Achim Prill 8, Jayson Punwani 28; Public Health Image Library: 17; Rex Features: Sedat Ozkomec 37; Science Photo Library: Mauro Fermariello 13, 39, 42, Steve Gschmeissner 11, Philippe Psaila 29, 41, Charles D Winters 14; Shutterstock: Carlos Arranz 18, Mario Bruno 24, Kevin L Chesson 6, Michael Coddington 36, Jarrod Erbe 26, Laurence Gough 45, Tom Grill 33, Tom Grundy 34, Ragne Kabanova 31, Jon Kroninger 16, Emin Kuliyev 5, Rob Marmion 4, Timothy R. Nichols 10, Rae 21, Supri Suharjoto 27, Derek Thomas 32, Vladimir Zivkovic 38.

Contents

Step inside

What would you see if you stepped inside a crime laboratory? Many scientific labs concentrate on one particular type of science, such as chemical analysis or plant biology. The equipment in each lab is suited for the type of work that is done there. Forensic science laboratories are not like this. Because so many different types of evidence are examined and analyzed in the forensic lab, it has the equipment to carry out a range of scientific tests.

Some of the types of evidence that are examined include:

- soil samples
- body tissues and fluids
- powders, tablets, and liquids
- paint fragments
- fibers
- explosives residue
- fingerprints, bite marks, and tire tracks
- firearms and tool marks.

Forensic scientists use powerful microscopes to look at materials in minute detail.

This forensic lab is packed with equipment that can analyze the evidence found at crime scenes.

Careful examination and analysis of this evidence can help to reveal details of a crime, the criminal, and sometimes the victim too.

Equipment

The type of equipment used depends on the evidence. A powerful microscope may be used to look at the structure of fibers. Special equipment may be used to carry out chemical analysis of a sample. Computers can be used to compare fingerprint details with national and international records. Special light sources can be used to search for traces of blood.

Many procedures carried out in the forensic lab need special chemicals. All will be carefully labeled and carry hazard warnings where necessary. Weighing scales might be needed to measure the amount of a powder that is to be used.

Protecting the evidence

Forensic scientists have to be very careful not to lose, destroy, or spoil any evidence. For example, they must avoid one of their own hairs becoming mixed with those in a sample. To minimize the risk of this happening, they usually wear protective clothing, latex gloves, and sometimes goggles in the laboratory.

Most forensic labs contain a wide variety of materials and equipment. They are often busy places, with many different investigations being carried out at the same time.

Fingerprints

A fingerprint is a mark that is made when a finger is pressed against something hard. The skin on our fingers is covered with lots of tiny ridges. These make a distinct pattern. Your fingerprint pattern is unique—nobody else's is exactly the same.

A long history

Fingerprints have been used for centuries. Over one thousand years ago, the Chinese used fingerprints on some documents instead of signatures. At the end of the 19th century, people in the West began to look at fingerprints. In 1892, Francis Galton published a method for analyzing fingerprints.

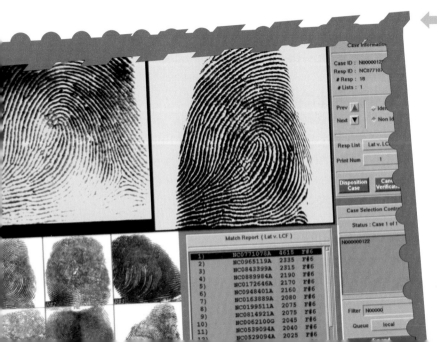

The police use computers to match prints found at a crime scene with those of known criminals.

Galton suggested his method should be used by detectives. Five years later, the Henry Classification System of fingerprint analysis was introduced. It was named after Sir Edward Richard Henry, who was in charge of the project.

In 1901, Scotland Yard set up the Fingerprint Bureau in England. Within five years, the New York City Police Department was also using fingerprinting to help identify criminals.

Types of fingerprints

There are three different types of fingerprints:

Patent prints are made when something wet or sticky is transferred from a fingerprint to a surface. Patent prints are easily seen and photographed.

Latent prints are made when natural body oils and sweat are transferred from a finger to a surface. Latent prints are not usually visible, but show up when a special powder or chemical is applied to the surface of the fingerprint.

Impressed prints are made when a finger is pressed into a soft material such as soap or wax. These prints are often visible and can be photographed.

TRUE CRIME...

The Rojas case

Juan Vucetich, an Argentine police official, made the first criminal fingerprint identification in 1892. He was able to identify Francesca Rojas, a woman who murdered her two young sons and then cut her own throat in an attempt to blame a man called Velasquez. Then a policeman noticed a bloody fingerprint on a doorframe at Francesca's house. He cut out the bloodied wood and took it to Juan Vucetich. Vucetich studied the fingerprints on the wood and compared them with the fingerprints of Francesca Rojas. The prints matched. Francesca Rojas was interviewed again, and this time she confessed.

7

loop

whorl

arch

IN DEPTH

Shapes in fingerprints

Three general shapes can be found in fingerprints. The word "LAW" can help you remember them:

L = Loops

A = Arches

W = Whorls

Loops cross the fingertip from side to side.

Whorls make circular or spiral patterns.

Arches slope up and down.

Scientists can begin to distinguish one print from another by comparing these shapes. They look at their number, size, pattern arrangement, and other details.

8

The arches and loops can easily be seen on this clear fingerprint.

Taking prints

In the early days of fingerprinting, prints from a suspect were taken by rolling each finger in turn over an inkpad and then pressing them down on a piece of paper. Scientists compared the prints by eye, perhaps using a magnifying glass to look at tiny details. It was often a slow, laborious process.

Modern computer technology has made fingerprinting much simpler and quicker. The person puts their finger on the surface of an electronic reader. An image of the fingerprint is captured by a digital scanner within a few seconds. The reader records the scan, and the information is saved onto a computer. The computer notes patterns on the fingerprints and searches for similar patterns in the fingerprint database, a digital collection of thousands or even millions of prints.

The first electronic fingerprint matching system was developed in the 1980s in Japan. It was called AFIS—Automated Fingerprint Identification Systems. Today, most countries have their own fingerprint identification system. They are linked together, so that fingerprints can be quickly compared against millions of records around the world.

Fingerprint matching can only be useful as evidence if it is accurate. To minimize the risk of incorrect matches being made, most countries have strict rules about how much information must be available. This is usually defined by the number of distinct features that must match between the two prints.

Fingerprint scanners are used to collect and compare fingerprints.

EXAMINE THE EVIDENCE

Take your own prints

You can take your own fingerprints. Rub a soft pencil on a piece of paper to make a very dark area. Rub one of your fingertips over this until it is covered in grey. Carefully apply a piece of sticky tape to your fingertip. Slowly pull off the tape and stick it onto a piece of plain white paper. Your fingerprint will show up clearly! Now ask a friend to make a fingerprint in the same way. Compare the two. Are they alike? Can you see loops, arches, and whorls?

9

Fibers

Fibers are fine threads or strands. They are everywhere. All sorts of things are made from fibers. Some are twisted together to make ropes, string, and twine. Some are woven together to make fabrics used for clothing, sheets, and cushion covers. Some are knotted together to make carpets and rugs.

Fibers as evidence

Fibers can be retrieved from crime scene surfaces such as floors and furniture. They can be taken from a victim's clothes and body. They can also be found on suspects' clothes, and in their cars and houses. If a fiber from a crime scene matches one from a suspect's clothing, it can help to prove the suspect was at the scene.

Analysis

It can be difficult to tell whether two fibers are the same just by looking at them. They may seem to have the same color and texture.

Scientists can make an initial examination of a fiber through a magnifying glass.

10

Electron microscopes

Forensic scientists sometimes use a powerful instrument to look at fibers: an electron microscope. Most microscopes use light to see a specimen. They can magnify things more than one thousand times. An electron microscope does not use light. Instead, it uses tiny particles called electrons. Some electron microscopes can magnify things two million times. At this intense magnification, amazingly tiny details can be seen. This allows for much more accurate fiber analysis.

The microscopic examination of a thread can determine where it was made.

When you look at fibers under a microscope, however, more details can be seen. Forensic scientists examine the shape, size, and appearance of the fiber. They also analyze the chemicals in the dye and the fiber itself.

Some fibers come from natural materials such as wool. Others are from synthetic (man-made) materials such as nylon. Modern technology allows forensic scientists to identify not just the type of fiber, but where it came from, what sort of fabric it was made into, and the manufacturer.

EXAMINE THE EVIDENCE

Collect fiber evidence

Choose a busy room in your house. Look for any loose fibers. If you find any, use a small piece of sticky tape to lift each one and stick it onto a piece of paper. How many different types of fibers can you find? Can you tell where they come from? Using a magnifying glass will help you to see more details.

Chemical analysis

In the forensic laboratory, scientists analyze samples to find out which chemicals they contain. A variety of different substances can be analyzed, including the following:

- body fluids, such as blood, saliva, and urine
- body samples, such as tissues and organs
- materials, such as clothing
- liquids, tablets, and powders

12

Crime scene investigators collect samples to take back to the lab.

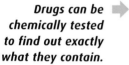

Drugs can be chemically tested to find out exactly what they contain.

Analysis of a sample can show whether or not it contains substances such as alcohol, drugs, dyes, paints, poisons, or explosives. Many forensic scientists specialize in one particular area. For example, forensic toxicologists analyze biological samples. Forensic metallurgists analyze metals.

The process of analysis

How does a forensic scientist analyze a sample? There are two main steps. First, all the different substances in the sample are separated. Then each substance is tested to find out what it is. Forensic scientists have some very sophisticated equipment to help them carry out these processes.

TRUE CRIME...

Lynn Turner

On March 2, 1995, in Cobb County, Georgia, a police officer named Maurice Glenn Turner began to feel ill. By the following day Turner was found dead. Doctors thought he must have died from heart problems. His wife, Lynn Turner, collected his life insurance money. Then, in 2001, Lynn Turner's new partner, Randy Thompson, also fell ill and then died. Again, Lynn Turner collected the life insurance money.

Turner's family thought it was odd that both men should have died in such similar ways. They asked the police to investigate the deaths and samples from both bodies were analyzed. They contained ethylene glycol, which is a chemical found in antifreeze. Lynn Turner was convicted of murdering the men by poisoning them both with antifreeze. Forensic toxicology provided the evidence that proved the men had been murdered.

13

Separating the chemicals

To analyze a sample, the different substances in it are separated from each other. This is usually done by chromatography.

↑ *Chromatography separation is used to find out exactly what components are in a mixture.*

In thin layer chromatography, a glass slide is coated with a thin layer of material such as silica gel. Tiny drops of the sample are put at one end of the gel. The slide is then put in a liquid, up to a point just below the drops on the slide. The liquid travels up the slide and carries the substances with it. Some substances are carried farther than others, so they are separated. The substances are often colorless and so cannot be seen. To make them show up, they can be viewed under ultraviolet light or sprayed with a special chemical.

In gas chromatography, a sample is diluted in a liquid such as chloroform or methanol. The solution is injected into an upright hollow tube. The tube is very hot inside, so the liquid evaporates very quickly. The sample travels through the column. Scientists can draw certain conclusions about the substances involved based on how quickly they travel through the column.

Thin layer chromatography and gas chromatography can help identify the substances in a sample. The results are compared with those of known chemicals. If they match, it is very likely that the chemicals are the same.

The chromatography equipment used in forensic labs used to be large and heavy. New, smaller, and lighter instruments have now been developed. Some government agencies, including the FBI, are already using these portable instruments. This means that forensic scientists can analyze samples found at the crime scene, without needing to send them back to the lab for testing, saving time and money.

EXAMINE THE EVIDENCE

Chromatography at home

You can try some chromatography for yourself. This method is just like thin layer chromatography but uses paper in place of silica gel. On a narrow strip of paper towel, draw a large dot with a water-soluble felt-tip pen about one inch up from the bottom. Wrap the other end of the paper towel around the middle of a pencil and secure it with paper clips. Put about half an inch of water in a jar. Balance the pencil on the top of the jar, so that the end of the paper towel just dips into the water. Make sure the ink dot is above the water level.

The water will travel slowly up the paper and carry the ink with it. Many inks are made up of several different colors. Because some colors travel further up the paper than others, they separate out. Eventually, the water will reach the top of the paper. Take the paper out of the water and leave it to dry. You will be able to see all the colors that the ink contained.

15

Analyzing the chemicals

Forensic scientists cannot always identify a chemical from the results of a chromatography separation. Then more tests are done using an instrument called a mass spectrometer. Usually, the chemicals are fed straight from the gas chromatography tube into the mass spectrometer. There they are bombarded with electrons. These high-energy particles break up the chemicals. Because every chemical breaks up in a different way, each one makes a unique pattern. The break-up pattern can be used to identify the chemical.

Scientists can view the break-up pattern on a screen. A computer can be used to compare details of break-up patterns from different samples. The break-up patterns and the comparison details can be printed onto paper as a permanent record of the results.

16

Samples to be analyzed are stored in sterile glass vials. It is important that the sample does not become contaminated. This would affect the analysis and make the result unusable.

IN DEPTH

Gunpowder residue

When a person is shot, a forensic chemist might use infrared light to examine a suspect's hands and clothing. Infrared light cannot be seen with the human eye, but it can make things that are invisible in ordinary light show up. If any gunpowder residue is present, it will show up in the infrared light. Samples of any residue found can then be analyzed. The residue on the bullet used in the shooting can also be analyzed. If the residues match, the evidence suggests that the suspect fired the bullet.

Sample integrity

Forensic chemists usually examine evidence in a sterile laboratory to minimize the risk of contamination. They also keep a document called a chain of custody. This document stays with the evidence at all times, and includes the signatures of everyone who touches it. The chain of custody acts as a record and makes it difficult to tamper with samples, which increases their reliability as evidence.

⬇ *This forensic scientist is using a mass spectrometer to analyze evidence.*

Mid-air explosion

On November 1, 1955, an airplane exploded shortly after taking off from Denver's Stapleton Airport. Forensic scientists examined thousands of pieces of the plane, its cargo, and the passengers' belongings. The residues they found suggested that the explosion had been caused by dynamite. One of the people who died in the explosion was Daisie King, the mother of a man called Gilbert Graham. During their investigations, the FBI found some bomb-making equipment at Graham's house. He eventually admitted that he had made the bomb and put it in his mother's luggage. The chemical analysis of the residue linked Graham to the crime.

17

Looking for drugs

In 2006, the FBI needed to trace a particular batch of illegal drugs. Other agencies sent them some candies that were suspected of containing these drugs, so that they could analyze them. These were the steps taken by the FBI:

1. The candies were mixed with a solution of sodium bicarbonate, which is a liquid in which they would dissolve.

2. The solution was then passed through filter paper.

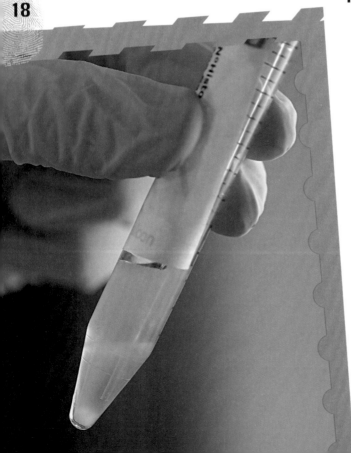

By mixing the candy with sodium bicarbonate, forensic scientists created a solution that could be easily analyzed.

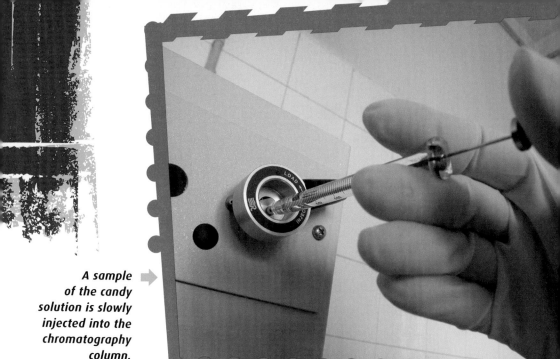

A sample of the candy solution is slowly injected into the chromatography column.

3. The filtered solution was mixed with chloroform and injected into a gas chromatography tube. Inside the tube, the liquid evaporated and the chemicals in the sample traveled through the column.

4. In gas chromatography, some chemicals travel through the column more quickly than others. When each chemical reached the end of the tube, they passed into a mass spectrometer. Here they were bombarded with electrons.

5. The electrons broke up the chemicals. The break-up pattern was shown on a screen.

6. The forensic scientists compared the break-up pattern with the patterns of known substances.

7. Success! The pattern from the sample was an exact match for an addictive drug called methaqualone. The chemical analysis proved that the candies did contain this illegal drug. The forensic evidence had provided vital information for their investigation.

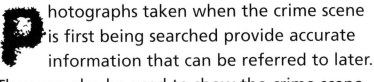
Photographic evidence

Photographs taken when the crime scene is first being searched provide accurate information that can be referred to later. They can also be used to show the crime scene to officers who did not see it for themselves. Witness statements can be checked against the photographs for confirmation.

Getting the best photographs

Different things will be photographed depending on the crime. If there is a body, it will be photographed to show where it was found. The photographs will also show what position the body was in, and whether any injuries were visible. They will provide a record of how items of clothing were arranged.

◀ *A police officer photographs evidence at a crime scene. The place in which evidence is found is marked with a number.*

Photographs of blood stains are taken so forensic scientists can study them.

Photographers use different equipment for different jobs. A wide-angle lens can be used to photograph an entire room. A high-powered lens might be used to photograph tiny details, such as blood splashes.

Bloodstains

Bloodstain patterns vary depending on what caused them. For example, blood simply dripping onto a surface from a shallow cut creates a very different pattern than blood spurting from a gunshot wound. Bloodstain pattern analysis is a very detailed process. It can provide vital information about the type of weapon used, the direction of the blow or gunshot, and the positions of the victim and the killer. Photographs of bloodstain patterns can be used in court as evidence of these facts.

21

Labeled markers and scales are put next to pieces of evidence before they are photographed. The markers are used to identify each piece of evidence. The scales are used to show the size of the evidence.

The autopsy

Forensic photographers usually attend an autopsy, in which a body is examined after death. They record the different stages of the autopsy from start to finish.

It is possible to change photographs, so the accuracy of forensic photographs could be doubted. To help ensure that they are not altered, each one is marked with the time and date when it was taken. This helps improve their chances of being accepted as evidence.

The letters "DNA" stand for DeoxyriboNucleic Acid. DNA is found in every living thing. Humans, like other living things, are made up of millions of tiny units called cells. Inside each cell is an even smaller part—the nucleus. Inside the nucleus are various structures, including pairs of threads called chromosomes. Individual sections of each chromosome are called genes. These genes are made from DNA. They carry information about us in a code called the genetic code.

Tiny cells, which can be seen only under a microscope, contain lots of DNA information.

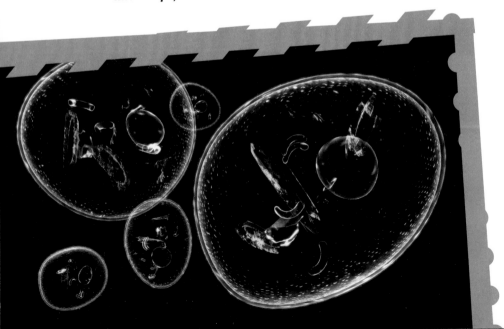

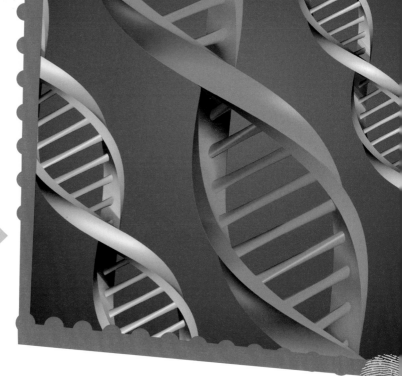

Two chemical strands twist together to form DNA, the code that determines how all life looks and functions.

What is DNA like?

DNA consists of two strands twisted together. The strands are linked by pairs of building blocks called bases. There are four different types of bases. The order in which the bases appear in the DNA makes up the genetic code for that individual. There are about 3 billion base pairs in the human genetic code, which can be arranged in countless different ways.

What does DNA do?

DNA allows the genetic code information to be passed from one generation to the next. You get half your genetic code from your mother and half from your father. This means that you can inherit characteristics from each of your parents.

Developing DNA analysis

Scientists worked out what the structure of DNA is like in 1953. It was not until about 30 years later that a British scientist, Alec Jeffreys, figured out a method for identifying a person from their DNA. Since it was first introduced in the 1980s, DNA analysis has become very important to forensic scientists. It is now a routine part of forensic investigations.

DNA can be extracted from old bones, which means that forensic scientists can help solve ancient crimes.

What can DNA tell us?

Analyzing a DNA sample can provide lots of information. The results can be used to answer questions such as:

IN DEPTH

Planted evidence

Although DNA can reveal invaluable clues about how a crime may have been carried out, police and forensic scientists are also aware that evidence can be "planted" to throw investigators off track. Criminals sometimes leave objects near a crime scene that carry DNA belonging to an innocent person. It is therefore vital that investigators use DNA analysis and the results it yields very carefully in every case.

• Was the suspect present at the crime scene? If DNA from a sample at the crime scene matches the DNA of the suspect, it strongly suggests that he was at the crime scene. However, unless the sample from the crime scene is specifically linked to the crime, such as being found on the murder weapon, it cannot prove the suspect committed the crime.

• What is the identity of the body?
When a body is found, DNA analysis can help the police discover who the person is. The DNA from members of the same family will all show some similarities. The DNA from a body can be compared with DNA from family members. If there are enough similarities, it suggests the person is from that family. The DNA from the body can also be compared with samples held on DNA databases. The body may be identified from this if the person had previously had a DNA sample analyzed by police.

Recent DNA analysis suggests that Dr. Crippen may not have murdered his wife—though he was hanged for the crime in 1910.

TRUE CRIME...

Dr. Crippen

The case of Dr. Crippen is a famous one. Cora Crippen, his wife, vanished. Some time later, the remains of a human body were found in a cellar at the Crippens' house in London, England. Police thought it must be Cora's body. Dr. Crippen was found guilty of poisoning her, and he was hanged in 1910. Recently, however, evidence has been found that suggests he might not have been guilty. Forensic scientists compared some DNA from the remains of the body with DNA from members of Cora's family. They were different enough to suggest strongly that the body found was not Cora's. So now there are two puzzles: if the body wasn't Cora, who was it? And what really happened to Cora? We still do not know.

25

DNA profiling is the process of comparing the patterns found in different samples of DNA to see if they match. ➡

What is used for DNA analysis?

DNA can be extracted from any biological material. This might be a hair, a piece of bone, or a drop of blood or saliva. Even the tiny amount of biological material in a fingerprint can yield DNA for analysis! The sample can be fresh or it can have been stored dry or frozen for many years. Once it has been collected from the crime scene, it is taken to the forensic laboratory. Then the process of analysis can begin.

26

Finding the match

Most human DNA is the same. Only 0.01 percent—or 1 part in every 10,000—is different. It is this tiny amount of DNA that forensic scientists work with. Several important regions, or markers, in the DNA have been found. These are used to help identify individuals. No single marker can identify a person. You can think of it like this: a witness saw a tall man at the crime scene. There are lots of tall men, so this information alone is not enough to help identify one specific person. If they saw a tall man with black hair and a large tattoo, that narrows the field down. The more features they saw, the more likely the identification is correct. With DNA analysis, the more markers that match, the more likely it is that two samples came from the same person.

In the US, 13 specific markers are typically used for DNA analysis.

DNA databases

DNA analysis can be useful if the police do not have a suspect. Information from all DNA samples that have been analyzed are stored in national and international databases. A sample from a crime scene can be compared to the data held on these databases. There might be a match to a person who has committed a previous crime. That would suggest that they are more likely to be guilty of the current crime.

IN DEPTH

Unreliable evidence?

In some countries, a method called low copy number DNA tests are used. This method is useful when only a tiny amount of DNA is found. Chemical copies of the DNA are made until there is enough to be analyzed. This seems like a good idea, but scientists found that mistakes can be made during the copying process. This means that the sample that is analyzed is slightly different from the original DNA. The argument about whether the low copy number DNA method is reliable enough to be used as evidence in court is still going on.

DNA profiles can be viewed by investigators on a DNA database.

Who is it?

The police need to know if DNA from a crime scene matches the DNA of their main suspect. Follow the steps in DNA analysis, from the crime scene to the final analysis.

1. A crime scene investigator carefully lifts a hair from the crime scene. She uses tweezers so that she does not touch the hair herself. She puts it into a sterile container and labels it.

2. The container is taken to the forensic laboratory. At the lab, the hair is removed from the sterile container. It is put in another container ready for the next step.

⬇ *As a centrifuge spins around at high speed, the force of the movement separates materials of different densities.*

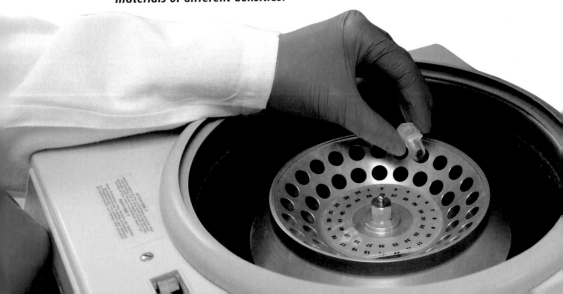

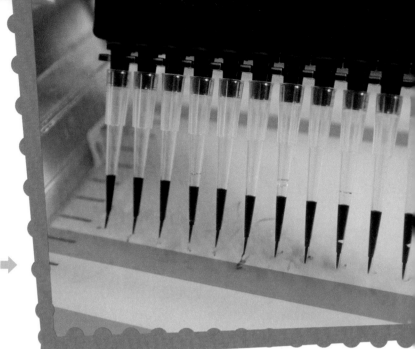

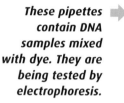

These pipettes contain DNA samples mixed with dye. They are being tested by electrophoresis.

3. The DNA is separated from everything else. Several different techniques are used in this process. They include the addition of chemicals to break open the cells, and then spinning the sample at very high speeds in a machine called a centrifuge.

4. Small sections of the DNA are copied many times using an enzyme called DNA polymerase. The process is called the polymerase chain reaction (PCR). Then a technique called electrophoresis is used, in which the copies are separated into individual groups by an electric current. Special dyes and chemicals are added that allow scientists to visualize the DNA markers.

5. The forensic scientist compares the crime scene DNA with the suspect's DNA. If there is no suspect, the DNA is compared with samples on a computer database. The more matching markers found between the samples, the greater the likelihood is that they came from the same person.

6. It appears that the DNA found at the crime scene matches the DNA of the main suspect!

Pathology

I t is part of the job of a forensic pathologist to examine the bodies of people who have died as the result of an accident, a crime, or suicide. The pathologist may also examine the wounds of living victims. From their investigations, they can provide information for the police about the number and type of injuries, the type of weapon used, the time of death, and the precise cause of death.

Autopsy

Examination of a dead body is called a post mortem, or autopsy. This is usually carried out at a morgue rather than in the forensic laboratory. However, body organs and fluids, as well as any trace evidence found on the body, may be sent to the lab for analysis. The main aim of an autopsy is to determine the cause and time of death.

Looking at the outside of the body

The body is weighed and measured. If possible, the victim's sex, race, and their estimated age are all recorded. Then the outside of the victim's body is examined very carefully. The pathologist records everything he or she finds and photographs are taken. Marks on the body, such as any needle marks, wounds, and bruises are examined and measured. Any trace evidence found, such as fibers under the fingernails, or fragments of paint in the hair, are removed and sent for analysis. These might help to identify the murderer.

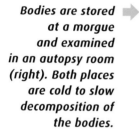
Bodies are stored at a morgue and examined in an autopsy room (right). Both places are cold to slow decomposition of the bodies.

Any dirt or soil found on the body is also sent for analysis. This might help to link the murder to a particular place. Bullet wounds are examined to uncover any fragments of the bullet.

In a murder investigation, a pathologist will examine the hands of the deceased for fingernail samples and other possible evidence. For example, traces of the murderer's skin may be left under the fingernails as the victim defends his or her body during the attack. This will yield valuable DNA for analysis.

IN DEPTH

Rigor mortis

When a person dies, some changes take place in their body. One of these affects the muscles. In a living person, the muscles become shorter when they contract and longer when they relax. These muscle actions pull on bones, allowing the person to move. After death, changes in the muscles make them rigid, so they cannot contract or relax. This rigidity is called rigor mortis. It begins three or four hours after death and usually lasts for about 24 hours. More changes in the muscles take place during this time and the stiffness gradually disappears. Rigor mortis can sometimes help forensic scientists to figure out the time of death to within a few hours.

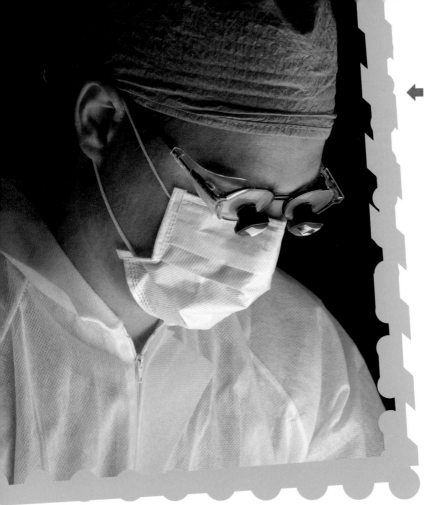

Pathologists are medical doctors who specialize in forensic pathology. Their job is to determine the cause and manner of death.

Looking inside the body

To examine the inside of the body, it is cut open. The first cut is large and Y-shaped. It runs diagonally from each shoulder to the breastbone, and then straight down to the groin. The skin and muscle are folded back so that the organs can be seen. The rib cage is cut open to show the organs inside the chest.

The pathologist records anything unusual, such as signs of disease or injury. Then he removes the internal organs one at a time. Each organ is weighed, and samples are sent to the laboratory to be analyzed. Samples of body fluids, such as blood and urine, are also sent for analysis.

Next the head and brain are examined for signs of damage or anything unusual, then the samples are sent for analysis.

IN DEPTH

Stomach contents

The contents of the stomach can provide answers to questions such as what foods the victim ate last, and how long before death they ate them. These can be important facts in a crime investigation. Imagine a person was seen eating a pizza in a restaurant at 8 p.m. The body of this person is found a couple of days later. If the stomach contents show that he or she ate pizza shortly before death, the victim probably died the same evening he or she was seen in the restaurant.

When the pathologist has finished examining the body and all the samples have been taken and taken for analysis, he or she will stitch the body back together again. The corpse is then stored in a large refrigerated compartment. When the police and forensic team are satisfied that their investigations are complete, the body can be sent to an undertaker for burial or cremation.

33

Forensic pathologists examine skin tissue through a microscope.

Teeth

Teeth are hard-wearing and remain in the skull long after death. Information from teeth can be used to identify both victims and criminals.

Identifying a victim

When you visit the dentist, he or she examines your teeth. They note any teeth that are missing, damaged, crowned, or filled. The information is recorded on your dental record. Although some dental records are still kept on paper, most are now stored on computers. If an unidentified body is found, the teeth can be compared with national dental records. This information can be used to find out who the person was.

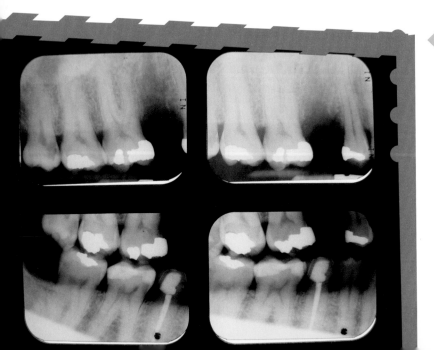

This person's dental X-rays show that a tooth is missing. This may help to identify a body.

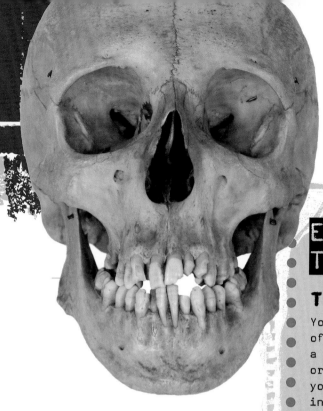

The teeth in this skull can be matched to dental records and help identify the victim.

35

Teeth remain fixed in the jawbone long after death. This means that they can be used to identify bodies of which nothing remains but a skeleton. They can also be used to identify badly burned or mutilated bodies.

Identifying a criminal

When a person bites something, their teeth leave a mark. People's jaws are different sizes, and everybody's teeth are different. This means that each person's bite mark is unique, and it can be used to identify them. If a person is bitten by someone else, the bite mark can be examined closely. If there is a suspect, a model called a cast can be made of his or her bite mark. Different materials are used to make bite mark casts, including rubber and plastic. The cast can then be compared to the bite mark on the victim. If there is no suspect, the bite mark can be compared with national and international dental records.

Guns and bullets

Ballistics is the study of guns and bullets. Forensic ballistics experts examine and analyze guns and bullets found at a crime scene. They also carry out more detailed analysis in the forensic laboratory. Their investigations can provide valuable information for police, such as matching a bullet with the gun that fired it.

36

Used bullets and cartridges can be analyzed to match them to the gun that fired them.

A ballistics expert examines a firearm used in a crime. He may fire the rifle in a safe environment to find out more information.

Marks on bullets

When a gun is fired, the bullet is marked by grooves in the barrel. Every gun has different grooves, which make a specific set of marks on the bullets fired from it.

Ballistics look at these markings. If police have found a gun that they suspect was involved in the crime, the ballistics experts may fire a bullet from it into a soft material that won't damage the bullet. Then they can compare the markings on the crime scene bullet with their test bullet. If the police have not found a gun, the bullet markings can be compared with records held on a database. It may be possible to identify the gun used from these records.

IN DEPTH

The BFB

The Bureau of Forensic Ballistics (BFB) was set up in 1925, in New York. Its aim was to provide ballistic analysis for police forces throughout the US. This was needed because few police forces had the experts who could carry out ballistics work. One of the people involved in the Bureau from the beginning was Calvin Goddard. He obtained information from many gun manufacturers and carried out test firings. It was the first step in the development of the amazing ballistics databases in use today.

Early ballistics

The first recorded case in which ballistics evidence helped to solve a crime was in London in 1835. A man had been shot and killed. A bullet in the form of a lead ball was found. Police suspected that the man's servant was the murderer. They examined the markings on the lead ball that killed the man. They also examined the piece of paper that made a seal between the ball and the gunpowder in the gun. They found that the paper had been torn from a newspaper in the servant's bedroom. When the police confronted the servant with this evidence, he confessed to the murder.

38

A bullet hole can tell experts a lot about the gun that fired the bullet.

Microscopes

The microscope is one of the most important instruments in ballistics investigations. Often the microscope is linked to a camera so that photographs can be taken of the bullet under view. The photographs can then be stored on a computer. The microscope may also be linked to closed circuit television, so that the evidence can be studied on a large screen.

Special microscopes called comparison microscopes are used. Comparison microscopes allow the scientist to view two different images side by side. One image may be of a bullet from a crime scene. The other image may be from a database. The scientist can compare the details, lining up the images to see how closely they match. If the two images are the same, it means the bullet has been fired from the same type of gun.

Gun crime experts

Ballistics experts may also examine the crime scene. Bullet holes in bodies and in the surrounding area can help to pinpoint where the gun was fired from. Other forensic experts may also be involved in the analysis of evidence related to gun crimes. These can include:

- forensic pathologist—examines bullet holes and powder burns on a body
- forensic metallurgist—analyzes the metal that bullets are made from
- forensic chemist—analyzes gunpowder residue.

Putting together the information from each of these experts can help the police build up a more complete picture of the crime, and it is all evidence that can be used to secure a conviction or prove innocence.

39

Experts can use a microscope to compare the markings on cartridges.

Identifying the gun

Follow a forensic scientist as they investigate whether the gun found in the main suspect's car is the one that fired the bullet retrieved from a crime scene.

1. A forensic scientist fires a bullet from the gun found in the suspect's car. The bullet is fired into a tank of water to prevent the bullet from being damaged in any way.

2. The bullet is recovered from the tank and taken to a comparison microscope.

Any gun found at the scene of a crime is sealed in a bag to preserve evidence.

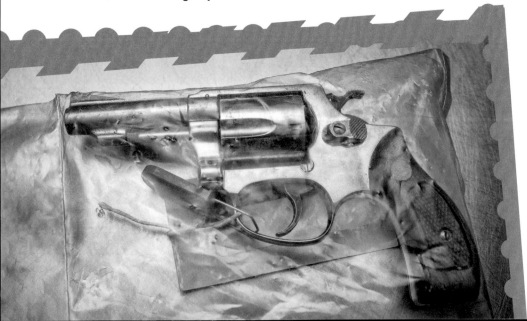

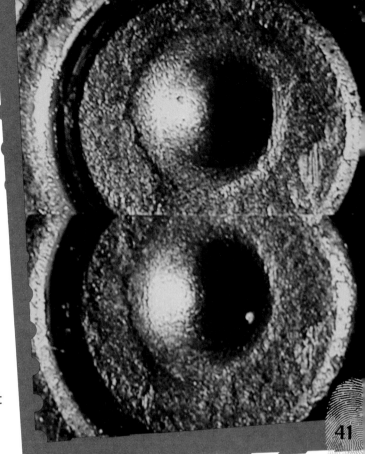

The make of a gun can be identified by analyzing the bullets shot from it. These two bullets were fired from the same gun.

3. The forensic scientist also examines the bullet found at the crime scene.

4. The two bullets are examined side by side under the microscope. They are rotated so their entire surfaces are viewed.

5. The microscope images are viewed on a screen. Marks on the bullets are compared.

6. The marks are lined up. They match exactly. A photograph is taken. This can be used in court as evidence that the gun was the one used to fire the bullet found at the crime scene.

7. The police do sometimes get things wrong. Freelance ballistic experts are sometimes hired by lawyers to review police records and evidence, in an attempt to unearth new information that might help a suspect prove his or her innocence.

Tool marks

Many kinds of tools might be used when a crime is committed. Tools may be used to force an entry into a building. They may be used as weapons. Luckily for police, most tools leave a mark of some kind. Different tools leave different marks. The marks can be used to identify the type of tool used. They may even be able to prove which particular tool it was.

Different marks

Marks are made when a tool moves over a surface. Several factors affect the type of mark that is made. These include the type of tool, the type of surface, the amount of force used, and the type of movement made. Tool marks can be made in several ways. The table on the next page shows some possible movements, surfaces, marks, and tools.

⬇ *The markings on this piece of bone were made by a knife.*

42

IN DEPTH

Features

Every tool has its own unique set of features. Each contributes in some way to the marks the tool makes. The features can be put into three groups:

Group features are shared by all tools of that type. For example, a group feature of a knife is that it has a handle and a blade.

Subgroup features are shared by some tools of that type, but not by all of them. For example, knives made by one manufacturer may all have wooden handles, but knives made by another manufacturer may all have plastic handles.

Individual features are unique to one particular tool. For example, a knife may have a nick or dent in the blade. No other knife will have exactly the same dent in exactly the same place.

When a tool is examined, the features will be considered in this order: first its group features, then its subgroup features, and finally its individual features.

43

What sort of movement was made?	What sort of surface was marked?	What sort of mark was made?	What sort of tool was used?
hitting	metal car	dents	baseball bat
sliding	skin	long scratch	knife
crushing	telephone wire	ends squashed together	wire cutters
back and forth movement	metal bar	series of similar teeth marks	saw

The marks made by a particular tool give the forensic scientist clues about the tool itself. Examination of the marks under a microscope will show tiny details that can be used to identify the exact tool used. This information can help forensic scientists prove that a tool was used to break into a building or cause a serious injury.

Careers in forensics

What would it be like to work in a forensic laboratory? That can depend on whether you specialize in a particular area of forensic science, or work in more general areas.

Qualifications

Most forensic scientists have a background in sciences such as chemistry and biology. At many colleges and universities, courses are offered in forensic science leading to certificates, diplomas, and degrees. Some courses cover all aspects of forensic science. Others are highly specialized. Different programs have different entry requirements, but for most a science background is required.

SALARY CHART

This chart shows what some forensic scientists working in the lab can expect to earn.

Forensic scientist	Approximate salary
Forensic pathologist	$120,000–$163,000
Chemist	$46,387–$75,431
Laboratory technician	$46,387–$75,431

Some forensic scientists qualify in a science subject and then have additional training to become a forensics expert. For example, a person who carries out forensic DNA analysis may have a degree in biology or genetics, then undertake more training to do forensic work in this specific field.

If you enjoy lab work, forensic science might be the career for you.

Not all forensic scientists have science backgrounds. For example, a forensic photographer may have trained in photography and then specialized in forensic work. Others may train first as police officers, working as crime scene investigators, and then move on to work in one particular area of forensic science, such as fingerprint analysis.

Qualities

There are several essential qualities you need for working in a forensics laboratory. To succeed, you need to:

- have a reasonable understanding of science
- work accurately and carry out scientific tests reliably and to a high standard
- be methodical and logical in the way you work, so that you do not mix up samples or results
- be able to concentrate on details and not miss anything
- be competent at math and computing so that you can analyze your data and write reports.

If this sounds like you, you might want to think about a career in the forensic lab.

Glossary

antifreeze—Chemical that is put into car radiators to prevent them from freezing in cold weather.

autopsy—Examination of a dead body to determine the cause of death.

ballistics—The study of firearms and bullets.

centrifuge—Instrument used for separating substances by spinning them at very high speeds.

chromatography—A method used for separating out the different chemicals in a substance.

chromosome—A strand of DNA.

contamination—When evidence is mixed up with unwanted substances.

database—Combined collection of data, or pieces of information.

DNA—The genetic material that carries the code that determines the makeup of every living thing.

electrophoresis—A method of separating substances that is used in the analysis of DNA.

fiber—Fine thread or strand.

forensic scientist—Person who uses science or technology to investigate and establish facts or evidence in a court of law.

genetic code—Code that carries information about us from one generation to the next.

infrared—Type of light invisible to our eyes, with wavelengths longer than visible red light.

mass spectrometer—Machine used for analyzing and separating chemicals.

microscope—Instrument used to magnify small objects so people can examine them.

morgue—Place where dead bodies are kept until they are identified or buried.

pathologist—Doctor who studies tissue and other parts of remains to help work out a history of disease, injury, or cause of death.

polymerase chain reaction (PCR)—Process that uses the DNA polymerase enzyme to copy sections of DNA so that they can be analyzed.

post mortem—Medical examination of a dead body.

residue—Something that is left behind.

rigor mortis—Stiffness of the body that begins three to four hours after death.

saliva—Liquid produced by glands in the mouth to keep it moist.

sterile—Free of living germs.

toxicologist—Scientist who deals with poisons and their effects.

ultraviolet—Type of light invisible to our eyes, with wavelengths shorter than visible violet light.

Further reading

Books

Beres, D. B., and Anna Prokos. *Dusting and DNA*. New York: Scholastic, 2008.

Hamilton, Sue. *DNA Analysis: Forensic Fluids and Follicles*. Abdo & Daughters, 2008.

Morrison, Yvonne. *The DNA Gave It Away!*. New York: Children's Press, 2008.

Wright, D. *Hair and Fibers*. New York: Sharpe Focus, 2008.

Web sites

This site includes everything you need to know about forensics and the science behind solving crimes:

www.discoverychannel.co.uk/crime/_home/index.shtml

This is the FBI web site, especially for kids. Play games, solve puzzles, take the Special Agent challenge, and much more at:

www.fbi.gov/kids/6th12th/6th12th.htm

Click on the links to look at the evidence behind the different crimes and use forensic science to help to catch the criminals.

www.trutv.com/forensics_curriculum

There is a database of forensic science facts, a timeline showing important forensic events, and a game to play, at:

www.virtualmuseum.ca/Exhibitions/Myst/en/rcmp/index.html

Index